GOD'S LITTLE INSTRUCTION BOOK

FOR THE CLASS OF **2011**

GOD'S LITTLE INSTRUCTION BOOK

FOR THE CLASS OF 2011

David C Cook

transforming lives together

GOD'S LITTLE INSTRUCTION BOOK FOR THE CLASS OF 2011
David C Cook
4050 Lee Vance View
Colorado Springs, CO 80918 U.S.A.

David C Cook Distribution Canada
55 Woodslee Avenue, Paris, Ontario, Canada N3L 3E5

David C Cook U.K., Kingsway Communications
Eastbourne, East Sussex BN23 6NT, England

David C Cook and the graphic circle C logo
are registered trademarks of Cook Communications Ministries.

Bible credits are located at the end of this book.

ISBN 978-1-4347-0063-6
eISBN 978-1-4347-0346-0

The Team: Ingrid Beck, Amy Kiechlin, Sarah Schultz, Jack Campbell
Interior Design: Karen Athen
Cover Design: studiogearbox.com
Cover Photo: Steve Gardner/Pixelworks Studio

Printed in the United States of America
First Edition 2009

1 2 3 4 5 6 7 8 9 10

123010

INTRODUCTION

Congratulations! As a member of the Class of 2011, you are part of a new and changing millennium filled with innovative technologies and amazing discoveries.

These exciting times have made the earth a much more challenging and complicated place to live. You will be confronted with opportunities to make wise decisions and to be a shining light in an often dark and confusing place. How do you make good choices when everything around you is moving and changing? And how do you cut through the hype and find what is good?

In *God's Little Instruction Book for the Class of 2011*, we offer you wisdom sufficient to help you navigate the twenty-first century. We have taken quotes from ordinary people and heroes throughout history and combined them with wisdom from the Bible to help you become the person you aspire to be. We hope the truths presented

FOR THE CLASS OF **2011**

in these pages will help you settle your life on an unshakable foundation and enable you to build a world filled with infinite possibilities.

Do not seek to follow in the footsteps of
the men of old; seek what they sought.
—Matsuo Basho

**I love everyone who loves me, and
I will be found by all who honestly
search.**

Proverbs 8:17 CEV

The future is as bright as the promises of God.
—WILLIAM CAREY

Whatever God has promised gets stamped with the Yes of Jesus.

2 Corinthians 1:20 MSG

The way to get to the top is to get off your bottom.
—DR. EUGENE SWEARINGEN

How long will you lie down, O sluggard? When will you arise from your sleep?

Proverbs 6:9 NASB

No person has the right to rain on your dreams.
—MARIAN WRIGHT EDELMAN

I can do all things through Christ who strengthens me.

Philippians 4:13 NKJV

We have a God who delights in impossibilities.
—Andrew Murray

Jesus said to them, "With people this is impossible, but with God all things are possible."

Matthew 19:26 NASB

You can give without loving, but you
cannot love without giving.
—Amy Carmichael

**It is more blessed to give than to
receive.**

Acts 20:35

FOR THE CLASS OF 2011

First keep the peace within yourself, then
you can also bring peace to others.
—THOMAS À KEMPIS

**Blessed are the peacemakers, for they
will be called sons of God.**

Matthew 5:9

He that has learned to obey will
know how to command.
—Solon

**The wise in heart accept commands,
but a chattering fool comes to ruin.**

Proverbs 10:8

FOR THE CLASS OF **2011**

Snuggle in God's arms. When you are hurting, when you feel lonely, left out. Let Him cradle you, comfort you, reassure you of His all-sufficient power and love.

—KAY ARTHUR

Let, I pray, Your merciful kindness be for my comfort.

Psalm 119:76 NKJV

FOR THE CLASS OF **2011**

At the height of laughter, the universe is flung
into a kaleidoscope of new possibilities.
—JEAN HOUSTON

**He will yet fill your mouth with
laughter and your lips with shouts of
joy.**

Job 8:21

FOR THE CLASS OF 2011

The future belongs to those who see possibilities before they become obvious.
—JOHN SCULLEY

The vision is yet for an appointed time.... It will surely come, it will not tarry.

Habakkuk 2:3 KJV

Our prayers must mean something to us
if they are to mean anything to God.
—Maltbie D. Babcock

**I thank You and praise You, O God of
my fathers, who has given me wisdom
and might and has made known to me
now what we desired of You.**

Daniel 2:23 AB

FOR THE CLASS OF **2011**

We never test the resources of God
until we attempt the impossible.
—F. B. MEYER

**Now faith is being sure of what we
hope for and certain of what we do not
see.**

Hebrews 11:1

To believe in God is to know that all the rules will be fair, and that there will be wonderful surprises!
—CORITA KENT

The Rock: His works are perfect, and the way he works is fair and just.

Deuteronomy 32:4 MSG

Kites rise highest against the wind, not with it.
—WINSTON CHURCHILL

When the way is rough, your patience has a chance to grow. So let it grow, and don't try to squirm out of your problems.

James 1:3–4 TLB

FOR THE CLASS OF **2011**

When you do the things you need to do when you need to do them, the day will come when you can do the things you want to do when you want to do them.

—ZIG ZIGLAR

He becometh poor that dealeth with a slack hand: but the hand of the diligent maketh rich.

Proverbs 10:4 KJV

FOR THE CLASS OF **2011**

Smart is believing half of what you hear;
brilliant is knowing which half to believe.
—AUTHOR UNKNOWN

**For wisdom will enter your heart, and
knowledge will fill you with joy.**

Proverbs 2:10 NLT

Don't fear change—embrace it.
—Anthony J. D'Angelo

I am leaving you with a gift—peace of mind and heart! And the peace I give isn't fragile like the peace the world gives. So don't be troubled or afraid.

John 14:27 TLB

FOR THE CLASS OF **2011**

The road to success is dotted with many tempting parking places.
—AUTHOR UNKNOWN

Let us throw off everything that hinders and the sin that so easily entangles, and let us run with perseverance the race marked out for us.

Hebrews 12:1

FOR THE CLASS OF 2011

School seeks to get you ready for examination; life gives the finals.
—Author unknown

Examine yourselves to see whether you are in the faith; test yourselves.

2 Corinthians 13:5

FOR THE CLASS OF **2011**

Always do right. This will gratify some people, and astonish the rest.

—MARK TWAIN

This is a trustworthy saying, and I want you to insist on these teachings so that all who trust in God will devote themselves to doing good. These teachings are good and beneficial for everyone.

Titus 3:8 NLT

FOR THE CLASS OF 2011

Work without a vision is drudgery; a vision without work is only a dream; work with a vision is victory.

—AUTHOR UNKNOWN

Work hard so God can say to you, "Well done." Be a good workman, one who does not need to be ashamed when God examines your work.

2 Timothy 2:15 TLB

FOR THE CLASS OF 2011

It's not hard to make decisions when
you know what your values are.
—Roy Disney

**Daniel purposed in his heart that he
would not defile himself.**

Daniel 1:8 KJV

I would rather fail in the cause that
someday will triumph than triumph in
a cause that someday will fail.
—WOODROW WILSON

**Thanks be to God who always leads us
in triumph in Christ.**

2 Corinthians 2:14 NKJV

FOR THE CLASS OF 2011

God loves each of us as if there were only one of us.
—St. Augustine

Christ's love compels us, because we are convinced that one died for all.

2 Corinthians 5:14

FOR THE CLASS OF **2011**

My faith isn't in the idea that I'm more moral than anybody else. My faith is in the idea that God and His love are greater than whatever sins any of us commit.
—RICH MULLINS

I sought the LORD, and he answered me; he delivered me from all my fears.

Psalm 34:4

FOR THE CLASS OF 2011

A true friend never gets in your way unless you happen to be going down.
—ARNOLD GLASOW

If one falls down, his friend can help him up. But pity the man who falls and has no one to help him up!

Ecclesiastes 4:10

Obedience to the call of Christ nearly always costs everything to two people: the one who is called, and the one who loves that one.

—OSWALD CHAMBERS

If you will indeed obey My voice and keep My covenant, then you shall be a special treasure to Me above all people; for all the earth is Mine.

Exodus 19:5 NKJV

FOR THE CLASS OF 2011

A man without mirth is like a wagon without springs, in which one is caused disagreeably to jolt by every pebble over which it turns.

—HENRY WARD BEECHER

A cheerful disposition is good for your health; gloom and doom leave you bone-tired.

Proverbs 17:22 MSG

FOR THE CLASS OF 2011

I count him braver who overcomes his desires
than him who conquers his enemies; for the
hardest victory is the victory over self.

—ARISTOTLE

I beat my body and make it my slave.

1 Corinthians 9:27

Trust in yourself and you are doomed to disappointment; ... but trust in GOD, and you are never to be confounded in time or eternity.
—DWIGHT L. MOODY

It is better to trust in the LORD than to put confidence in man.

Psalm 118:8 NKJV

A knowledge of the Bible without a college course is more valuable than a college course without the Bible.
—WILLIAM LYON PHELPS

All scripture is given by inspiration of God, and is profitable for doctrine, for reproof, for correction, for instruction in righteousness: That the man of God may be perfect, thoroughly furnished unto all good works.

2 Timothy 3:16–17 KJV

FOR THE CLASS OF **2011**

Never be afraid to trust an unknown
future to a known God.
—CORRIE TEN BOOM

**I will turn the darkness into light
before them and make the rough places
smooth.**

Isaiah 42:16

Success consists of getting up just
one more time than you fall.
—OLIVER GOLDSMITH

**I can do everything through him who
gives me strength.**

Philippians 4:13

FOR THE CLASS OF **2011**

You are only what you are when no one is looking.
—ROBERT C. EDWARDS

Not by way of eyeservice, as men-pleasers, but as slaves of Christ, doing the will of God from the heart.

Ephesians 6:6 NASB

Death is more universal than life. Every man dies; not every man really lives.
—WILLIAM WALLACE

I have come that they may have life, and have it to the full.

John 10:10

Little minds are tamed and subdued by misfortune; but great minds rise above them.
—WASHINGTON IRVING

A just man falleth seven times, and riseth up again.

Proverbs 24:16 KJV

Perseverance is a great element of success. If you only knock long enough and loud enough at the gate, you are sure to wake up somebody.

—HENRY WADSWORTH LONGFELLOW

Ask and it will be given to you; seek and you will find; knock and the door will be opened to you.

Luke 11:9

One of life's great rules is this: The more you give, the more you get.
—WILLIAM H. DANFORTH

The generous will prosper; those who refresh others will themselves be refreshed.

Proverbs 11:25 NLT

To trust in Him when no need is pressing, when things seem going right of themselves, may be harder than when things seem going wrong.

—GEORGE MACDONALD

Give me neither poverty nor riches, but give me only my daily bread. Otherwise, I may have too much and disown you and say, "Who is the LORD?" Or I may become poor and steal, and so dishonor the name of my God.

Proverbs 30:8–9

FOR THE CLASS OF **2011**

Shoot for the moon. Even if you miss,
you'll land among the stars.
—LES BROWN

Aim for perfection.

2 Corinthians 13:11

The great rule of moral conduct is,
next to God, to respect time.
—JOHANN KASPAR LAVATER

In all your getting, get understanding.

Proverbs 4:7 NKJV

FOR THE CLASS OF **2011**

I am only one; but still I am one. I cannot do everything, but still I can do something; … I will not refuse to do the something I can do.
—HELEN KELLER

Under [Christ's] direction the whole body is fitted together perfectly, and each part in its own special way helps the other parts.

Ephesians 4:16 TLB

FOR THE CLASS OF 2011

Anything I've ever done that ultimately was worthwhile initially scared me to death.
—C. S. Lewis

I would have despaired unless I had believed that I would see the goodness of the LORD in the land of the living.

Psalm 27:13 NASB

Relying on God has to begin all over again
every day as if nothing had yet been done.
—C. S. LEWIS

**For such is God, our God forever, and
ever; He will guide us until death.**

Psalm 48:14 NASB

No matter what a man's past may
have been, his future is spotless.
—JOHN R. RICE

**Forgetting those things which are
behind, and reaching forth unto those
things which are before.**

Philippians 3:13 KJV

Do not borrow trouble by dreading tomorrow. It is the dark menace of the future that makes cowards of us all.
—DOROTHY DIX

For he will order his angels to protect you wherever you go.

Psalm 91:11 NLT

Remember not only to say the right thing in the right place, but far more difficult, to leave unsaid the wrong thing at the tempting moment.

—BENJAMIN FRANKLIN

Careful words make for a careful life; careless talk may ruin everything.

Proverbs 13:3 MSG

FOR THE CLASS OF 2011

I think the one lesson I have learned is that there is no substitute for paying attention.
—DIANE SAWYER

We must pay more careful attention, therefore, to what we have heard, so that we do not drift away.

Hebrews 2:1

Every job is a self-portrait of the person who does it. Autograph your work with excellence.
—AUTHOR UNKNOWN

Daniel was preferred above the presidents and princes, because an excellent spirit was in him.

Daniel 6:3 KJV

When we long for life without difficulties, remind us that oaks grow strong in contrary winds and diamonds are made under pressure.
—PETER MARSHALL

But you must learn to endure everything, so that you will be completely mature and not lacking in anything.

James 1:4 CEV

The happiest people don't necessarily have the best of everything. They just make the best of everything.
—AUTHOR UNKNOWN

I have learned the secret of being content in any and every situation.

Philippians 4:12

FOR THE CLASS OF 2011

Blessed is the man who finds out which way God is moving and then gets going in the same direction.

—AUTHOR UNKNOWN

Whether you turn to the right or to the left, your ears will hear a voice behind you, saying, "This is the way; walk in it."

Isaiah 30:21

Nothing is ever lost by courtesy.... It pleases him who gives and him who receives, and thus, like mercy, it is twice blessed.

—Erastus Wiman

While we have opportunity, let us do good to all people.

Galatians 6:10 NASB

Every calling is great when greatly pursued.
—OLIVER WENDELL HOLMES

I press toward the mark for the prize of the high calling of God in Christ Jesus.

Philippians 3:14 KJV

FOR THE CLASS OF 2011

Here's the key to success and the key to failure: we become what we think about.

—EARL NIGHTINGALE

Whatever is true, whatever is noble, whatever is right, whatever is pure, whatever is lovely, whatever is admirable—if anything is excellent or praiseworthy—think about such things.

Philippians 4:8

The heights by great men reached and kept
Were not attained by sudden flight,
But they, while their companions slept,
Were toiling upward in the night.
—HENRY WADSWORTH LONGFELLOW

So let's not get tired of doing what is good. At just the right time we will reap a harvest of blessing if we don't give up.

Galatians 6:9 NLT

FOR THE CLASS OF **2011**

Courage is resistance to fear, mastery
of fear—not absence of fear.
—MARK TWAIN

**Yea, though I walk through the valley
of the shadow of death, I will fear no
evil: for thou art with me; thy rod and
thy staff they comfort me.**

Psalm 23:4 KJV

FOR THE CLASS OF **2011**

Whatever you dislike in another person,
take care to correct in yourself.
—THOMAS SPRAT

**Why do you look at the speck of
sawdust in your brother's eye and pay
no attention to the plank in your own
eye?**

Matthew 7:3

Sainthood lies in the habit of referring
the smallest actions to God.
—C. S. LEWIS

**Praise Him for His mighty acts;
praise Him according to His excellent
greatness!**

Psalm 150:2 NKJV

FOR THE CLASS OF 2011

Do exactly what you would do if you felt most secure.
—MEISTER ECKHART

Have not I commanded you? Be strong, vigorous, and very courageous. Be not afraid, neither be dismayed, for the Lord your God is with you wherever you go.

Joshua 1:9 AB

You may be disappointed if you fail, but you are doomed if you don't try.

—BEVERLY SILLS

The sluggard craves and gets nothing, but the desires of the diligent are fully satisfied.

Proverbs 13:4

FOR THE CLASS OF 2011

The world wants your best, but God wants your all.
—AUTHOR UNKNOWN

Thou shalt love the Lord thy God with all thy heart, and with all thy soul, and with all thy mind.

Matthew 22:37 KJV

Real prayer comes not from gritting
our teeth but from falling in love.
—Richard Foster

**By day the Lord directs his love, at
night his song is with me—a prayer to
the God of my life.**

Psalm 42:8

Carve your name on hearts and not on marble.
—CHARLES H. SPURGEON

The only letter I need is you yourselves! ... They can see that you are a letter from Christ, written by us ... not one carved on stone, but in human hearts.

2 Corinthians 3:2–3 TLB

FOR THE CLASS OF **2011**

It is impossible for that man to despair who remembers that his Helper is omnipotent.
—JEREMY TAYLOR

I will lift up my eyes to the mountains; from where shall my help come? My help comes from the LORD, who made heaven and earth.

Psalm 121:1–2 NASB

This world belongs to the man who is wise enough to change his mind in the presence of facts.
—ROY L. SMITH

Whoever heeds correction gains understanding.

Proverbs 15:32

We too often love things and use people, when we should be using things and loving people.

—AUTHOR UNKNOWN

Love each other with genuine affection, and take delight in honoring each other.

Romans 12:10 NLT

FOR THE CLASS OF **2011**

Where fear is present, wisdom cannot be.
—Lucius C. Lactantius

The LORD is my light and my salvation—whom shall I fear?

Psalm 27:1

The world is governed more by
appearance than realities.
—DANIEL WEBSTER

**These are a shadow of the things that
were to come; the reality, however, is
found in Christ.**

Colossians 2:17

Never despair; but if you do, work on in despair.
—TERENCE

As for you, be strong and do not give up, for your work will be rewarded.

2 Chronicles 15:7

When you are laboring for others, let it be with the same zeal as if it were for yourself.
—AUTHOR UNKNOWN

Put yourself aside, and help others get ahead. Don't be obsessed with getting your own advantage. Forget yourselves long enough to lend a helping hand.

Philippians 2:4 MSG

FOR THE CLASS OF 2011

The most important single ingredient in the formula of success is knowing how to get along with people.
—THEODORE ROOSEVELT

See that no one pays back evil for evil, but always try to do good to each other and to everyone else.

1 Thessalonians 5:15 TLB

FOR THE CLASS OF 2011

Life can only be understood backwards;
but it must be lived forwards.
—SØREN KIERKEGAARD

This is what the LORD says—your
Redeemer, the Holy One of Israel: "I
am the LORD your God, who teaches
you what is best for you, who directs
you in the way you should go."

Isaiah 48:17

FOR THE CLASS OF 2011

Success is never final; failure is never fatal; it is courage that counts.
—WINSTON CHURCHILL

Be of good courage, and he shall strengthen your heart, all ye that hope in the LORD.

Psalm 31:24 KJV

To love what you do and feel that it matters—
how could anything be more fun?
—KATHERINE GRAHAM

For my heart rejoiced in all my labour.

Ecclesiastes 2:10 KJV

FOR THE CLASS OF **2011**

When you were born, you cried and the world rejoiced. Live your life in such a way that when you die, the world cries and you rejoice.

—INDIAN PROVERB

For to me, living means living for Christ, and dying is even better.

Philippians 1:21 NLT

The secret of success is to do the
common things uncommonly well.
—JOHN D. ROCKEFELLER JR.

**Do you see a man who excels in his
work? He will stand before kings; he
will not stand before unknown men.**

Proverbs 22:29 NKJV

FOR THE CLASS OF 2011

The cheerful man will do more in the same time, will do it better, will preserve it longer, than the sad or sullen.

—Thomas Carlyle

When a man is gloomy, everything seems to go wrong; when he is cheerful, everything seems right!

Proverbs 15:15 TLB

Only passions, great passions, can
elevate the soul to great things.
—DENIS DIDEROT

Fervent in spirit; serving the Lord.

Romans 12:11 KJV

FOR THE CLASS OF **2011**

The greater part of our happiness or misery depends on our disposition and not our circumstances.

—MARTHA WASHINGTON

I know how to live on almost nothing or with everything. I have learned the secret of contentment in every situation.

Philippians 4:12 TLB

Don't be discouraged; everyone who got
where he is, started where he was.

—AUTHOR UNKNOWN

**Though your beginning was
insignificant, yet your end will increase
greatly.**

Job 8:7 NASB

FOR THE CLASS OF 2011

Prayer is an invisible tool which is
wielded in a visible world.
—ED COLE

**The weapons of our warfare are not
carnal, but mighty through God to the
pulling down of strong holds.**

2 Corinthians 10:4 KJV

FOR THE CLASS OF 2011

The ripest peach is highest on the tree.
—James Whitcomb Riley

Let us not become weary in doing good, for at the proper time we will reap a harvest if we do not give up.

Galatians 6:9

. It is amidst great perils we see brave hearts.
—Jean-François Regnard

Then I'm up again—rested, tall and steady, fearless before the enemy mobs coming at me from all sides.

Psalm 3:6 MSG

FOR THE CLASS OF 2011

An error doesn't become a mistake
until you refuse to correct it.
—ORLANDO A. BATTISTA

**He who heeds discipline shows the way
to life, but whoever ignores correction
leads others astray.**

Proverbs 10:17

Hating people is like burning down
your own house to get rid of a rat.
—HARRY EMERSON FOSDICK

**If you are always biting and devouring
one another, watch out! Beware of
destroying one another.**

Galatians 5:15 NLT

FOR THE CLASS OF 2011

When you flee temptations, don't
leave a forwarding address.
—AUTHOR UNKNOWN

**Now flee from youthful lusts and
pursue righteousness ... with those
who call on the Lord from a pure heart.**

2 Timothy 2:22 NASB

We live in deeds, not years; in thoughts, not breaths.… We should count time by heart throbs. He most lives who thinks most, feels the noblest, acts the best.

—ARISTOTLE

"In him we live and move and have our being." As some of your own poets have said, "We are his offspring."

Acts 17:28

Good nature begets smiles, smiles beget friends, and friends are better than a fortune.

—DAVID DUNN

The light in the eyes [of him whose heart is joyful] rejoices the hearts of others.

Proverbs 15:30 AB

Children who bring honor to their parents
reap blessings from their God.
—AUTHOR UNKNOWN

**Honor your father and your mother, so
that you may live long in the land the
LORD your God is giving you.**

Exodus 20:12

Laughter is the sun that drives
winter from the human face.
—Victor Hugo

**A merry heart maketh a cheerful
countenance: but by sorrow of the
heart the spirit is broken.**

Proverbs 15:13 KJV

It's a good thing to have all the props pulled out from under us occasionally. It gives us some sense of what is rock under our feet, and what is sand.

—MADELEINE L'ENGLE

He is the Rock, his works are perfect, and all his ways are just. A faithful God who does no wrong, upright and just is he.

Deuteronomy 32:4

FOR THE CLASS OF 2011

A good reputation is more valuable than money.
—Publilius Syrus

A good name is rather to be chosen than great riches.

Proverbs 22:1 KJV

I don't know the secret to success, but the key to failure is trying to please everyone.
—BILL COSBY

Am I now trying to win the approval of men, or of God?

Galatians 1:10

The greatest use of life is to spend it
for something that will outlast it.
—WILLIAM JAMES

**Store your treasures in heaven, where
moths and rust cannot destroy, and
thieves do not break in and steal.**

Matthew 6:20 NLT

FOR THE CLASS OF **2011**

Laziness is often mistaken for patience.
—FRENCH PROVERB

Let us throw off everything that hinders and the sin that so easily entangles, and let us run with perseverance the race marked out for us.

Hebrews 12:1

It isn't your problems that are bothering you.
It is the way you are looking at them.
—EPICTETUS

**Now we see through a glass, darkly;
but then face to face: now I know in
part; but then shall I know even as also
I am known.**

1 Corinthians 13:12 KJV

FOR THE CLASS OF 2011

The mind grows by what it feeds on.
—J. G. HOLLAND

The mind controlled by the Spirit is life and peace.

Romans 8:6

One man with courage makes a majority.
—AUTHOR UNKNOWN

Be strong and courageous. Do not be afraid or terrified because of them, for the LORD your God goes with you; he will never leave you nor forsake you.

Deuteronomy 31:6

Vision is the world's most desperate need. There are no hopeless situations, only people who think hopelessly.

—WINIFRED NEWMAN

Where there is no vision, the people perish.

Proverbs 29:18 KJV

FOR THE CLASS OF 2011

Once a word has been allowed to escape, it cannot be recalled.

—HORACE

Do not let any unwholesome talk come out of your mouths, but only what is helpful for building others up according to their needs, that it may benefit those who listen.

Ephesians 4:29

FOR THE CLASS OF **2011**

Obstacles are those frightful things you see
when you take your eyes off your goal.
—HENRY FORD

**We know that in all things God works
for the good of those who love him,
who have been called according to his
purpose.**

Romans 8:28

It often happens that those of whom we speak
least on earth are best known in heaven.
—Nicolas Caussin

You are the ones chosen by God, chosen for the high calling of priestly work, chosen to be a holy people, God's instruments to do his work and speak out for him.

1 Peter 2:9 MSG

FOR THE CLASS OF **2011**

Motivation is when your dreams put on work clothes.
—BENJAMIN FRANKLIN

Whatever you do, work at it with all your heart, as working for the Lord, not for men.

Colossians 3:23

FOR THE CLASS OF 2011

A good listener is not only popular everywhere,
but after a while he gets to know something.
—WILSON MIZNER

**The ear that hears the rebukes of life
will abide among the wise.**

Proverbs 15:31 NKJV

FOR THE CLASS OF 2011

The capacity to care is what gives
life its deepest significance.
—PABLO CASALS

**Bear one another's burdens, and
thereby fulfill the law of Christ.**

Galatians 6:2 NASB

FOR THE CLASS OF **2011**

The only way to have a friend is to be one.
—RALPH WALDO EMERSON

A man that hath friends must [show] himself friendly.

Proverbs 18:24 KJV

I am an old man and have known a great many troubles, but most of them never happened.
—MARK TWAIN

In peace I will lie down and sleep, for you alone, O LORD, will keep me safe.

Psalm 4:8 NLT

FOR THE CLASS OF 2011

The future belongs to those who believe
in the beauty of their dreams.
—ELEANOR ROOSEVELT

Anything is possible if you have faith.

Mark 9:23 TLB

God takes life's pieces and gives us unbroken peace.
—W. D. GOUGH

The peace of God, which surpasses all understanding, will guard your hearts and minds through Christ Jesus.

Philippians 4:7 NKJV

Jumping to conclusions is not half as good an exercise as digging for facts.

—Author unknown

Do your best to present yourself to God as one approved, a workman who does not need to be ashamed and who correctly handles the word of truth.

2 Timothy 2:15

He who created us without our help will
not save us without our consent.
—St. Augustine

**If you confess with your mouth, "Jesus
is Lord," and believe in your heart that
God raised him from the dead, you will
be saved.**

Romans 10:9

You can accomplish more in one hour with
God than one lifetime without Him.

—AUTHOR UNKNOWN

With God all things are possible.

Matthew 19:26 KJV

FOR THE CLASS OF 2011

Forgiveness means giving up your
right to punish another.
—DENNIS RAINEY

**But when you are praying, first forgive
anyone you are holding a grudge
against, so that your Father in heaven
will forgive your sins, too.**

Mark 11:25 NLT

FOR THE CLASS OF **2011**

Within your heart
Keep one still, secret spot
Where dreams may go
And, sheltered so,
May thrive and grow.
—Louise Driscoll

Above all else, guard your heart, for it is the wellspring of life.

Proverbs 4:23

People are lonely because they build
walls instead of bridges.
—JOSEPH NEWTON

**You should be like one big happy
family ... loving one another with
tender hearts and humble minds.**

1 Peter 3:8 TLB

There is no poverty that can overtake diligence.
—Japanese proverb

Sloth makes you poor; diligence brings wealth.

Proverbs 10:4 MSG

FOR THE CLASS OF **2011**

Many receive advice; only the wise profit by it.
—PUBLILIUS SYRUS

Pride only breeds quarrels, but wisdom is found in those who take advice.

Proverbs 13:10

FOR THE CLASS OF 2011

Opportunities are seldom labeled.
—JOHN A. SHEDD

Seek, and ye shall find; knock, and it shall be opened unto you.

Matthew 7:7 KJV

FOR THE CLASS OF **2011**

Unless you try to do something beyond what you have already mastered, you will never grow.

—RONALD E. OSBORN

Brethren, I do not regard myself as having laid hold of it yet; but one thing I do: forgetting what lies behind and reaching forward to what lies ahead, I press on toward the goal for the prize of the upward call of God in Christ Jesus.

Philippians 3:13–14 NASB

FOR THE CLASS OF **2011**

Before you borrow money from a friend,
decide which you need more.
—AUTHOR UNKNOWN

If a man borrows an animal from his neighbor and it is injured or dies while the owner is not present, he must make restitution.

Exodus 22:14

The Bible has a word to describe
"safe" sex: It's called marriage.
—GARY SMALLEY & JOHN TRENT

Honor marriage, and guard the sacredness of sexual intimacy between wife and husband. God draws a firm line against casual and illicit sex.

Hebrews 13:4 MSG

Never fear shadows. They simply mean
there's a light shining somewhere nearby.

—RUTH E. RENKEL

**Yea, though I walk through the valley
of the shadow of death, I will fear no
evil: for thou art with me.**

Psalm 23:4 KJV

FOR THE CLASS OF 2011

Let us not say, "Every man is the architect of his own fortune," but let us say, "Every man is the architect of his own character."

—GEORGE DANA BOARDMAN

I will never concede that you are right; I will defend my integrity until I die. I will maintain my innocence without wavering. My conscience is clear for as long as I live.

Job 27:5–6 NLT

The Bible knows nothing of a hierarchy of labor. No work is degrading. If it ought to be done, then it is good work.

—AUTHOR UNKNOWN

To rejoice in his labour; this is the gift of God.

Ecclesiastes 5:19 KJV

FOR THE CLASS OF 2011

Diligence is the mother of good fortune.
—CERVANTES

The plans of the diligent lead to profit.

Proverbs 21:5

'Tis better to be alone than in bad company.
—GEORGE WASHINGTON

Do not be misled: "Bad company corrupts good character."

1 Corinthians 15:33

I like the dreams of the future better
than the history of the past.

—BENJAMIN FRANKLIN

Forget about what's happened; don't keep going over old history. Be alert, be present. I'm about to do something brand-new. It's bursting out! Don't you see it?

Isaiah 43:18–19 MSG

FOR THE CLASS OF **2011**

You can lead a boy to college, but
you cannot make him think.
—KIN HUBBARD

**It is senseless to pay tuition to educate
a rebel who has no heart for truth.**

Proverbs 17:16 TLB

The little troubles and worries of life may be as stumbling blocks in our way, or we may make them stepping-stones to a nobler character and to Heaven. Troubles are often the tools by which God fashions us for better things.

—HENRY WARD BEECHER

No discipline is enjoyable while it is happening—it's painful! But afterward there will be a peaceful harvest of right living for those who are trained in this way.

Hebrews 12:11 NLT

FOR THE CLASS OF 2011

God never put anyone in a place
too small to grow in.
—AUTHOR UNKNOWN

**Give thanks in all circumstances, for
this is God's will for you in Christ
Jesus.**

1 Thessalonians 5:18

Maturity doesn't come with age; it comes
with acceptance of responsibility.
—ED COLE

**When I was a child, I spoke as a child,
I understood as a child, I thought as a
child; but when I became a man, I put
away childish things.**

1 Corinthians 13:11 NKJV

FOR THE CLASS OF **2011**

You must have long-range goals to keep you
from being frustrated by short-range failures.

—CHARLES C. NOBLE

**Let us fix our eyes on Jesus, the author
and perfecter of faith, who for the
joy set before him endured the cross,
scorning its shame, and sat down at
the right hand of the throne of God.**

Hebrews 12:2

FOR THE CLASS OF 2011

Many men have too much willpower.
It's *won't* power they lack.

—AUTHOR UNKNOWN

**A man without self-control is as
defenseless as a city with broken-down
walls.**

Proverbs 25:28 TLB

Politeness goes far, yet costs nothing.

—SENECA

A kind man benefits himself.

Proverbs 11:17

FOR THE CLASS OF **2011**

Most of the things worth doing in the world had been declared impossible before they were done.
—LOUIS D. BRANDEIS

Jesus looked hard at them and said, "No chance at all if you think you can pull it off yourself. Every chance in the world if you trust God to do it."

Matthew 19:26 MSG

FOR THE CLASS OF 2011

Keep your fears to yourself, but share
your inspiration with others.
—ROBERT LOUIS STEVENSON

**Honor Christ and let him be the Lord
of your life. Always be ready to give an
answer when someone asks you about
your hope.**

1 Peter 3:15 CEV

FOR THE CLASS OF 2011

Life is a coin. You can spend it any way you wish, but you can spend it only once.
—LILLIAN DICKSON

It is appointed unto men once to die, but after this the judgment.

Hebrews 9:27 KJV

FOR THE CLASS OF **2011**

Truth, like surgery, may hurt, but it cures.
—HAN SUYIN

Speaking the truth in love, we will in all things grow up into him who is the Head, that is, Christ.

Ephesians 4:15

Don't count on your education to make you wise.

—AUTHOR UNKNOWN

He who trusts in himself is a fool, but he who walks in wisdom is kept safe.

Proverbs 28:26

Most of the verses written about praise in God's Word were voiced by people faced with crushing heartaches, injustice, treachery, slander, and scores of other difficult situations.

—JONI EARECKSON TADA

David sang to the LORD ... when the LORD delivered him from the hand of all his enemies.... He said: "The LORD is my rock, my fortress and my deliverer."

2 Samuel 22:1–2

FOR THE CLASS OF **2011**

You can't test courage cautiously.
—ANNIE DILLARD

Whatever you do, do it heartily, as to the Lord and not to men.

Colossians 3:23 NKJV

The stars are constantly shining, but often we do not see them until the dark hours.

—AUTHOR UNKNOWN

My help comes from the LORD, the Maker of heaven and earth.

Psalm 121:2

I have decided to stick with love. Hate
is too great a burden to bear.
—MARTIN LUTHER KING JR.

Do everything in love.

1 Corinthians 16:14

To believe in something, and not
to live it, is dishonest.
—Mahatma Gandhi

**If we live by the Spirit, let us also walk
by the Spirit.**

Galatians 5:25 NASB

Some debts are fun when you are acquiring them,
but none are fun when you set about retiring them.
—OGDEN NASH

Why do you spend money for what is not bread, and your wages for what does not satisfy? Listen carefully to Me, and eat what is good, and delight yourself in abundance.

Isaiah 55:2 NASB

In His will is our peace.
—Dante Alighieri

**Great peace have those who love
Your law, and nothing causes them to
stumble.**

Psalm 119:165 NKJV

I am convinced that faith sometimes means knowing God can, whether or not He does.
—BETH MOORE

The God we worship can save us from you and your flaming furnace. But even if he doesn't, we still won't worship your gods and the gold statue you have set up.

Daniel 3:17–18 CEV

Let your words be the genuine picture of your heart.
—JOHN WESLEY

My mouth shall speak wisdom, and the meditation of my heart shall give understanding.

Psalm 49:3 NKJV

Call on God, but row away from the rocks.
—HUNTER S. THOMPSON

**Wisdom and good judgment
live together, for wisdom knows
where to discover knowledge and
understanding.**

Proverbs 8:12 TLB

We need to pay more attention to how we
treat people than to how they treat us.
—JOYCE MEYERS

**Love others as well as you love
yourself.**

Mark 12:31 MSG

FOR THE CLASS OF **2011**

The more I study nature, the more I stand amazed at the work of the Creator.

—Louis Pasteur

I consider thy heavens, the work of thy fingers, the moon and the stars, which thou hast ordained.

Psalm 8:3 KJV

FOR THE CLASS OF 2011